GICMP PROPHETIC BOOTCAMP
TRAINING MANUAL

Dwann Holmes

© 2021

By Dwann Holmes

ISBN:

All rights reserved. No portion of this book may be reproduced, stored in a retrieval system, or transmitted in any form or by any means—electronic, mechanical, photocopy, recording, scanning, or other—except for brief quotations in critical reviews or articles, without the prior written permission of the author.

Unless otherwise noted, all scriptures are taken from the King James Version.

Scriptures marked KJV are taken from the KING JAMES VERSION (KJV): KING JAMES VERSION, public domain.

Scripture taken from the New King James Version®. Copyright © 1982 by Thomas Nelson. Used by permission. All rights reserved.

Scripture quotations marked HCSB are taken from the Holman Christian Standard Bible®, Copyright © 1999, 2000, 2002, 2003, 2009 by Holman Bible Publishers. Used by permission. Holman Christian Standard Bible®, Holman CSB®, and HCSB® are federally registered trademarks of Holman Bible Publishers.

Scripture taken from *The Message*. Copyright © 1993, 1994, 1995, 1996, 2000, 2001, 2002. Used by permission of NavPress Publishing Group.

Scriptures have also been taken from the Bible Gateway website: www.biblegateway.com

Table of Contents

Setting the Foundation
- Objectives
- Introduction
- Course Curriculum Matrix

Leading In: Focus on the Facilitator
- Rationale for a Facilitator-Focused Curriculum
- Curriculum Matrix for the Facilitator
- First Reflection
- Course Vision
- Course Planning Guide
- Prayer Points

Preparing the Facilitator to Lead: Focus on Prophetic Bootcamp 101
- Module 1 Overview
- Module 2 Overview
- Module 3 Overview
- Module 4 Overview
- Mid-Course Reflection

Preparing the Facilitator to Lead: Focus on Prophetic Bootcamp 201
- Module 5 Overview
- Module 6 Overview
- Module 7 Overview
- Module 8 Overview

Leading Out: Focus on the Facilitator
    Facilitator's Evaluation
    Final Reflection

SETTING THE FOUNDATION

Objectives

- Provide the tools to facilitate the *GICMP Prophetic Bootcamp 101 & 102* courses.
- Impart the foundational principles and protocols every prophet should know.
- Encourage reflection and spiritual development through a facilitator-focused curriculum.
- Create a vision, planning guide, and prayer points for the training.

Introduction

Be diligent to present yourself approved to God,
a worker who does not need to be ashamed,
rightly dividing the word of truth.
2 Timothy 2:15 (NKJV)

It takes a strong knowledge of the Word and a faithful, intimate walk with God to train prophets at different stages in their prophetic journey. Prophetic destiny comes with a weighty mantle that requires a commitment to the Father's business, a willingness to submit, a determination to stop running from the call, and a humility to embrace your path fully.

Paul fathered and trained many sons and daughters in the faith. His life was a prophetic and apostolic bootcamp shared in Acts and the majority of the New Testament that he co-authored with the Holy Spirit. His nuggets of wisdom and insight to Timothy are exercises for you and your class to reflect on and complete.

The principles and protocols shared in these eight (8) modules are a result of my experience in training, mentoring, and serving as a spiritual mother and an apostle to many prophets. As you journey through the facilitation of this course, reflect on your journey to becoming a prophet or a prophetic voice. Recall how it felt to grow through the beginning, intermediate, and advanced stages of the prophetic walk. What wisdom nuggets can you share with your participants?

In preparation for the course, read over the training manual prayerfully and reflectively. Be intentional in seeking the Lord for His direction. Follow Paul's advice:

- **Be diligent** in presenting yourself approved unto God as His chosen vessel for training His prophets.
- **Put Him first** in all of your planning and training.
- **Be teachable** as a daily, diligent disciple of His word.
- **Rightly divide** His truth as you mine the scriptures for the following:
    a. Insights
    b. Revelations
    c. Prophetic Principles and Protocols
    d. Strategies and Action Plans

The *GICMP Prophetic Bootcamp Training Manual* will assist you in your facilitation of the course. It serves two purposes:
    (1) a **curriculum** to direct your focus, assist your planning, and guide your reflection. It includes the following:
- Rationale for a Facilitator-Focused Curriculum

- Curriculum Matrix for the Facilitator
- First Reflection
- Course Vision
- Course Planning Guide
- Prayer Points
- Mid-Course Reflection
- Facilitator's Evaluation
- Final Reflection

(2) a **guide** to help you lead your ministry through the training by mapping out the course through a course curriculum matrix and providing module overviews that include the following:
- Objectives
- Key Terms, Concepts, and Scriptures
- Lesson Structure and Discussion Questions
- Module Assignment and Rubric
- Facilitation Strategies, Supplemental Exercises, and Wisdom Nuggets

This manual emphasizes **discussion, application, self-assessment, practice**, and **reflection** as key tools in your facilitation of this course. It is highly recommended that you and your ministry keep journals during this training. Let's begin by reviewing the course curriculum matrix.

COURSE CURRICULUM MATRIX

	MODULES	CONCEPTS	ASSIGNMENTS	ASSIGNMENT OUTCOMES
PROPHETIC BOOTCAMP 101	**Module 1** The State and Purpose of Prophetics	Prophetics Perversion Genuineness & Authenticity of the Prophet Kingdom Versus Worldly Prophetics	1-Page Reflection	Reflect on their response to defending prophetics biblically and their call to prophetics as well as assessing their confidence in hearing the Lord and declaring His word.
	Module 2 The Purpose of Prophecy and the Prophet	Low-Level Prophetics Prophetic Activation Types of Prophets The Prophet as God's Representative	1-Page Report	Assess their ability to biblically prophesy. Research and reflect on the word study of the Hebrew word *nabi*.
	Module 3 The Purpose of God's Prophet	The Purpose of What God's Prophet Does Mantles & Mantle Distribution	1-Page Report	Identify biblical prophets' mantles, their distributions, and the opposition to their mantles. Assess their own prophetic mantles.
	Module 4 Knowing the Purpose of Prophetic Protocol	Prophetic Protocol & Prophetic Companies Organizational Models	Prophetic Reflection	Assess their progress in the prophetic.

COURSE CURRICULUM MATRIX

	MODULES	CONCEPTS	ASSIGNMENTS	ASSIGNMENT OUTCOMES
PROPHETIC BOOTCAMP 201	**Module 5** Understanding Your Prophetic Status *2 videos*	Review key concepts from Prophetic Bootcamp 101 Corporate Prophecy Psychic Versus Prophet	1-Page Report	Assess the global ramifications of worldly representations (including psychic TV shows) in various media outlets.
	Module 6 Prophesy Like a Prophet *2 videos* ***Note:** Modules 7 & 8 are on the next page.	Principles and Protocols of Prophesying the Word of the Lord Principles and Protocols of Entering the Next Dimension Quantum Physics Shift	Prophetic Philosophy	Explain the foundational, scripture-based principles on which their prophetic ministry stands. Discuss what God has ordained for their prophetic ministry to illuminate about the prophetic and the negative elements in the earth realm that God has called them to de-construct through their prophetic mantles. Briefly account for "what the prophetic is" and "what the prophetic isn't".

	Module 7 Prophetic Consecration for Preparation	Prophetic Consecration & Preparation Giving a Word to the Body Putting Suffering into the Proper Perspective	Continue working on Prophetic Philosophy	Outcomes remain the same.
	Module 8 Developing Your Prophetic Philosophy	Kingdom Initiative Prophetic Kingdom Ambassador Final Prophetic Principles and Protocols Looking Forward	Share Prophetic Philosophy	Present prophetic philosophies and receive feedback.

LEADING IN:
FOCUS ON THE FACILITATOR

Rationale for a Facilitator-Focused Curriculum

*The appearance of the wheels and their craftsmanship
was like the gleam of beryl, and all four had the same form.
Their appearance and craftsmanship [were] like a wheel within a wheel.
Wherever the Spirit wanted to go, the creatures went in the direction
the Spirit was moving. The wheels rose alongside them,
for the spirit of the living creatures was in the wheels.
Ezek.1:16,20 (HCSB)*

Facilitators learn with their participants. They lead with a servant's heart and model the same expectation that they desire to see: a teachable spirit. Leaders and their ministries are a fitly joined unit where each person walks in agreement and uses his or her gifts to accomplish the vision (Eph. 4:16).

The facilitator-focused curriculum emphasizes leading by example through reflection and placing the Holy Spirit at the center of everything you do.

Before you begin this training, you need to *lead in*:

- ASSESS where you are.
- CREATE your vision.
- DEVISE a plan for facilitation.
- DEVELOP prayer points.
- REFLECT on where you are and where you want to be.

After the training ends, you need to *lead out*:

- EVALUATE your facilitation.
- ASSESS if you met your vision and your prayer points.
- REFLECT on your steps in moving forward.

Curriculum Matrix For The Facilitator

PROPHETIC BOOTCAMP 101	LEADING IN:	THE PROCESS	LEADING OUT:	PROPHETIC BOOTCAMP 201
	LEADING IN: Focus on the Facilitator First Reflection Course Vision Course Planning Guide Prayer Points	**Preparing the Facilitator to Lead: Focus on the Course** 8 Module Overviews • Objectives • Key Terms • Key Concepts • Key Scriptures • Lesson Structure & Discussion Questions • Module Assignment & Rubric • Facilitation Strategies • Supplemental Exercises • Wisdom Nuggets • Mid-Course Reflection ⟵ CONTINUOUS REFLECTION AND PRAYER ⟶	**LEADING OUT:** Focus on the Facilitator Facilitator's Evaluation Final Reflection	

First Reflection

Write your responses to the following reflective questions in your journal.

1. **Your Intimacy with God**
    a. Take a few moments to find a quiet place where you can hear God's voice. Write what you hear and see.

2. **Your Facilitation Skills**
    a. Ask the Holy Spirit how He wants you to facilitate. Pray for Him to reveal the needs of your church, city, or region.
    b. What are your thoughts about facilitating the training?
    c. What are you most excited about when you think about the upcoming training?
    d. What do you think will be the most challenging aspect of the upcoming training?
    e. What is your facilitation style?
    f. What are your strengths as a facilitator?
    g. Which areas of growth do you want to improve?
    h. Reflect on Gen.1:11 & 1Cor.3:6. What seeds of instruction can you plant through your facilitation? How do you perceive your role as a facilitator: to plant or to water? How will you self-assess your effectiveness?

3. **Your Foundation in Prophetics**
    a. How do you define prophetics?
    b. What does that definition look like in action?
    c. How were you trained in prophetics?
    d. What is your prophetic philosophy?

4. **Your Lifestyle as a Prophet**
    a. How have you been maintaining your lifestyle as a prophet?
    b. How have your mantle, mandate, and mission changed?
    c. What challenges are you facing?
    d. In which areas do you need to grow?
    e. In what areas do you need to increase in strength and stamina?
    f. How do you prophetically transition well? Meditate on your transitions so far and think about what principles, protocols, wisdom, and insight you can share with your participants.
    g. What do you hope to gain from this course?

5. **Your Experiences in Prophetics**
    a. Reflect on 2 Tim. 2:15. Write your insights and revelations about this verse.
    b. How do you rightly divide the word as a prophet? How does this verse relate to prophets-in-training?
    c. What strategies, insights, experiences, and testimonies can you share with your participants?
    d. How can you connect your experiences to the principles of prophetics taught in this course?
    e. How have you effectively discerned the connections between what is going on in the spirit realm and what is manifesting in earth realm? What insights can you give your participants about those experiences?
    f. Have you ever served in a prophetic company? Reflect on your experiences and what you can share during this training.

6. **Your Ministry, Church, or Organization**
    a. What do you want your ministry, church, organization to gain from this course?
    b. How do you envision this course as a tool to become a stronger and more effective ministry, church, or organization?
    c. What areas do you foresee needing further development?
    d. What significant shifts do you hope will occur in your ministry, church, or organization?

7. **Your Region**
    a. What are the areas of need for your city, state, or region?
    b. How can this course help you meet those needs?
    c. How do you foresee the course causing a shift in your territory?

Course Vision

*If people can't see what God is doing, they stumble all over themselves.
But when they attend to what he reveals, they are most blessed.
Proverbs 29:18 (MSG)*

Reflect on the following prompts and respond to them in your journal.

1. Prepare to write your vision for this training by answering these questions:

    a. What is the Holy Spirit revealing to you?
    b. After taking this course, what changes or growth do you expect to see in your ministry, church, or organization?
    c. What do you want the prophetic to look like in your ministry, church, or organization after completing this course?
    d. How do you envision teaching, nurturing, and activating your participants during this course?
    e. How do you envision developing a company of prophets in your church, ministry, or organization?

2. Now write your vision statement.

3. List three (3) goals you want to accomplish by the end of this course.

4. What are the core values that define your ministry, church, or organization?

5. How do your vision statement, goals, and core values align with each other and this course?

Course Planning Guide

Reflect on the following information and write your course plan in your journal.

1st –Decide on Your Mode of Facilitation

- *Suggested Facilitation Mode:*

    Show the video and engage in discussion after viewing it.

- *Suggested Time Frame for Each Module:*

    The course is designed for you to cover the modules on a weekly basis.

- *Things to Consider during the Planning Phase:*

    This training manual provides you with module overviews. Each module overview has a lesson structure that outlines the order of activities in the video and includes additional discussion questions.

    Each module also has an assignment to complete. There is a one-page assignment sheet that provides instructions and a rubric for grading. You have the option of printing the assignment sheet and distributing it to your participants. Supplemental exercises and wisdom nuggets exercises are one-page, printable assignments that you have the option to assign. You will find them in Modules 1-3 & 5-6.

    Ask yourself:

    a. Where am I going to conduct the training: face-to-face, Zoom, Google Meet, Microsoft Teams, Adobe Connect, etc.?
    b. What facilitation mode will work best for my ministry, church, or organization?
    c. What equipment and other materials do I need to run the training?
    d. Do I want to cover each module weekly, bi-weekly, or monthly?
    e. How much time do I want to schedule for each session?
    f. How often do I want to meet?
    g. How will my participants submit assignments to me?
    h. Do I want to give the key scriptures as a homework assignment before we begin each module?
    i. How will I assess mastery of each module?

j. How do I want to handle our Q &A sessions and homework reviews? Do I want to discuss them before the video, after they take place in the video, or after the video has ended?
k. Do I want to find a platform that offers online discussions and have them engage in discussions virtually?
l. How will I take note of insight and revelations about each participant? How will I provide opportunities for them to further develop their prophetic gifts?

2nd –Decide on Materials for Your Ministry or Church

- *Things to Consider:*
    a. Journals
    b. Access to a computer, laptop, or mobile device
    c. Ask yourself:
        1. What else will my participants need to be successful in this training?
        2. What other systems do I need in place to facilitate effectively?

Prayer Points

It is important to pray targeted, effective prayers before, during, and after your training. Think of five (5) prayer points that you want to focus on while you facilitate. Write your prayer points, prayers, declarations, and decrees in your journal.

1st Prayer Point:_____

2nd Prayer Point:_____

3rd Prayer Point:_____

4th Prayer Point:_____

5th Prayer Point:_____

PREPARING THE FACILITATOR TO LEAD:
FOCUS ON PROPHETIC BOOTCAMP 101

Module 1 Overview

The State and Purpose of Prophetics

Objectives

In this module, participants will

1. Know the state of prophetics, foundational scriptures of prophetics, and the purpose of prophetics.

2. Reflect on their response to defending prophetics biblically and their call to prophetics as well as assessing their confidence in hearing the Lord and declaring His word.

Key Term

Prophetics

Additional Terms

False Humility
Motive
Perversion
Kingdom Prophetics
Worldly Prophetics
Genuineness/Authenticity
of the Prophetic

Key Concepts

Know the State of Prophetics
Know the Foundational Scriptures of Prophetics
Know the Purpose of Prophetics

Key Scriptures

Amos 3:7
2 Chr.20:20
1 Sam.9:7,9
Eph.2:19-20
Eph.4:7-13
1 Cor.14:1-5
1 Kgs.13:11-26

Module 1 Lesson Structure

1. Begin with the following discussion questions:

    - How would you define the term *prophetics*?
    - What does it look like in action?
    - What are your thoughts on the state and purpose of prophetics?
    - What do you expect its basic components to be?

    *Based on their responses, assess where they are and what you need to emphasize during the lesson.

2. Start Module 1 video.

3. Begin with introducing the three things prophets must know about prophetics: its state, its foundational scriptures, and its purpose.

4. Define the key term: *prophetic*. ***Note:** Definition comes from Paula Price's *The Prophet's Dictionary* (a foundational prophetic resource). ***

5. Share perspective on the state of prophetics.

6. Provide time for Q & A.

7. Read and discuss Amos 3:7, 2 Chr.20:20, 1Sam.9:7,9, Eph.2:19-20, Eph.4:7-13, 1 Cor.14:1-5, and 1 Kgs. 13:11-26.

8. Provide time for Q & A.

9. Ask the following discussion questions:

    - Have you ever had a time when you felt like your prophetic gift was rejected? How did you deal with it?
    - What can you do to maintain the purity of your prophetic voice?

10. Explain homework assignment.

11. Provide additional time to address questions in the chat:

    - *1st Participant's Question*: How do you know when to accept gifts after giving a prophecy yet not wanting to exploit the gift of prophecy?
    - *2nd Participant's Question*: Is sowing into a prophet similar to a pastor's love offering?

    ***Note:** You may want to pause the video before the participants in the video ask the questions. Discuss the questions with your participants and then listen to the video discussion. ***

12. End in prayer.

13. Debrief the video.

Module 1 Assignment

Write a 1-page reflection on the following questions. Include scriptural references in your responses.

- *Defense of the Prophetic*
  What is the quality of your ability to biblically DEFEND Prophetics as you know it?

- *Defense of Your Call to the Prophetic*
  What is the quality of your ability to DEFEND your call to Prophetics?

- *Confidence in Hearing God's Voice & Declaring His Word*
  How confident are you in hearing and DECLARING the voice of the Lord?

Rubric		
Criteria	Met the Criteria (Y)	Did Not Meet the Criteria (N)
• Explains the quality of their ability to biblically defend Prophetics with scriptural references.		
• Discusses the quality of their ability to defend their call to Prophetics with scriptural references.		
• Describes their assessment of their confidence in hearing and declaring the Word of the Lord.		
• Meets the 1-page requirement.		

Facilitation Strategies

*Then opened he their understanding,
that they might understand the scriptures.
Luke 24:45*

1. Compare and contrast biblical examples of kingdom prophetics and worldly prophetics in a group discussion. Here are some suggestions: Moses & Balaam, Samuel & the Witch of Endor, and Jeremiah & Hananiah.

2. If you are conducting the session on Zoom, you can also use breakout rooms. Divide your participants into groups and assign each group a pair of prophets (one representing kingdom prophetics and the other one representing worldly prophetics). Have each group discuss the similarities and differences between the two prophets. When everyone returns to the main room, ask each group to give feedback on the activity. Assess whether they know how to identify both types of prophetics.

3. Discuss your current protocols for declaring the Word of the Lord and engaging in prophetics. Assess what is working and what should change in order to meet God's agenda and your current needs.

4. You may want to assign the following supplemental exercise: *My Position in the Prophetics.*

5. You may want to complete the wisdom nuggets exercise together as a class or assign it as an individual activity.

My Position in the Prophetics

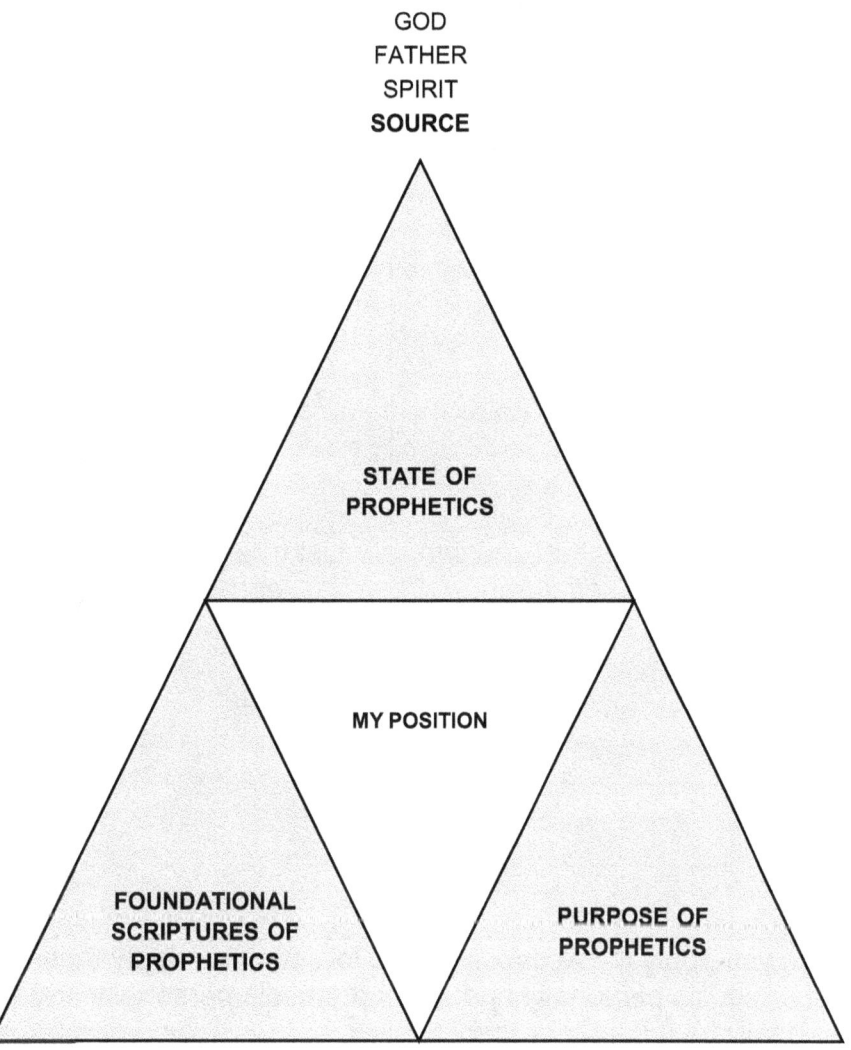

Reflective Question:

Where am I positioned in the current state,
foundational scriptures, and purpose of prophetics?

Wisdom Nuggets
1 Timothy 1:4-5, 12-18

	FOR THE LEADER OR MENTOR	FOR THE PROPHET-IN-TRAINING
PRINCIPLES	List three (3) principles that you can learn from these scriptures.	List three (3) principles that you can learn from these scriptures.
PROTOCOLS	List three (3) protocols that you can learn from these scriptures.	List three (3) protocols that you can learn from these scriptures.
APPLICATION	How can you apply these principles and protocols personally and professionally as a leader or mentor?	How can you apply these principles and protocols personally and professionally as a prophet?

Module 2 Overview

The Purpose of Prophecy and the Prophet

<u>Objectives</u>

In this module, participants will

1. Know the purpose of prophecy and the prophet.
2. Go through a prophetic activation.
3. Understand the difference between basic prophecy and prophesying like a prophet.
4. Differentiate between a church prophet and a global prophet.
5. Learn about different types of prophets.
6. Conduct a word study on the Hebrew word *nabi*.
7. Reflect on their ability to biblically prophesy.

<u>Key Terms</u>
Prophecy
Prophesy
Prophet
Nabi
Hozeh
Chozeh

<u>Additional Terms</u>
Edify
Exhort
Comfort
Mantle
Church Prophet
Global Prophet

Key Concepts

Basic Prophecy
Low-Level Prophetics
Prophesying Like a Prophet
Prophet as God's Representative

Key Scripture

1 Cor.14:1-5

Module 2 Lesson Structure

1. Begin with the following discussion questions:

   - Name one prophet from the Bible and share your thoughts about his or her purpose as a prophet.
   - How did this prophet defend his or her call to prophecy?

2. Start Module 2 video.

3. Begin with prayer and time for participants to share their comments or feedback about Module 1. ***Note**: You can also use this time to have them share their feedback on the homework assignment. ***

4. Introduce the module's topic: Know the Purpose of Prophecy & Know the Purpose of the Prophet.

5. Ask the following discussion question:

   - Think about what you know about prophecy. What is your definition of prophecy?

   *Based on their responses, assess where they are and what you need to emphasize during the lesson.

   *Pause the video before the participant gives her definition of prophecy and ask your class this question. Play the video after your discussion.

6. Define prophecy.

7. Read and discuss 1Cor.14:1-5. ***Note:** Make sure your participants have a clear understanding of what *edify, exhort, and comfort* mean. Ask them to give you definitions and examples. Ask them what makes each one different. ***

8. Explain that prophecy is low-level prophetics and list ten (10) things that it does.

9. Emphasize the purpose of the training is to teach, nurture, and activate.

10. Go through a prophetic activation using scripture for a given scenario and give feedback on the protocol for prophesying with scriptures:

    - **Step 1** (Basic Prophecy/Low-Level Prophetics): Give the scenario. Ask them to share what they would do and what scriptures they would use to prophesy.
    - **Step 2** (Basic Prophecy/Low-Level Prophetics): Tell them to declare and decree from their scriptures.
    - **Step 3** (Prophesying Like a Prophet): Speak on behalf of God by using "I" as they declare and decree.
        - **Example (Isa.26:3):** "I, the Lord God, will grant you perfect peace as you keep your mind on Me." Emphasize that this step will take them into another level of relationship and grace.

11. Listen to a seasoned prophet demonstrate how to prophesy using scripture for a different scenario.

12. Introduce second topic: Know the Purpose of God's Prophet. Define key terms: *prophet, nabi, hozeh,* and *chozeh*.

13. Identify five (5) representations of God that the prophet demonstrates: His arm, His voice, His mouth, His thoughts, and His will.

14. Show ways the prophet shows up in scripture and distributes from his or her mantles. Differentiate between the church prophet and the global prophet.

15. Explain the homework assignment.
16. Provide time for Q & A.

    - *1st Participant's Question:* How do we gain access to slides and videos?
    - *2nd Participant's Question:* What is the difference in the prophetic gifting found in the office of an apostle and the office of a prophet?

***Note:** You may want to pause the video before the participant in the video asks the second question. Discuss the question with your participants and then listen to the video discussion. ***

17. End in prayer.

18. Debrief the video.

Module 2 Assignment

Write a 1-page report on the following questions. Include scriptural references in your responses.

- *Self-Assessment*
  What is the quality of your ability to biblically prophesy?

- *Word Study*
  Do a word study on the Hebrew word *nabi*.

Rubric		
Criteria	Met the Criteria (Y)	Did Not Meet the Criteria (N)
• Explains the quality of their ability to biblically prophesy using specific examples and scriptural references.		
• Discusses their interpretation of the Hebrew meaning of *nabi* using scriptural references.		
• Shares personal insights and revelations from their study of the Hebrew word *nabi*.		
• Meets the 1-page requirement.		

Facilitation Strategies

*Then opened he their understanding,
that they might understand the scriptures.
Luke 24:45*

1. Provide opportunities after the second demonstration of prophesying for your participants to practice prophesying from scriptures. Have a list of scriptures to assign individually, in pairs, or in groups. Take them through the steps taught by Apostle Dwann. If you are in Zoom, use breakout rooms.

2. Here is a list of resources for prophetic activations, dreams, and chozeh prophets:

    - *You Can Prophesy: A Prophetic Pocket-Guide of Proven Strategies and Instructions on How to Release Personal and Corporate Prophecy* by Dwann Holmes

    - *You Can Interpret Your Dreams: A Prophetic Pocket Guide of Proven Spiritual Strategies to Accurately Help You Understand Your Dreams* by Dwann Holmes

    - *Prophetic Activation: Break Your Limitation to Release Prophetic Influence* by John Eckhardt

    - *GICMP School of the Seer* course

3. Discuss different examples of prophets in the Bible who demonstrated the many ways they functioned as God's representative in the earth. Use the list provided in the module.

4. Have participants show their understanding of the different types of prophets by identifying which ones are nabi, hozeh, or chozeh.

5. You may want to assign the following supplemental exercise: *My Mantle, My Mandate, & My Mission.*

6. You may want to complete the wisdom nuggets exercise together as a class or assign it as an individual activity.

My Mantle, My Mandate, & My Mission

*Cry aloud, spare not,
lift up thy voice like a trumpet.*
Isa.58:1a

<u>My Reflection</u> (Meditation) Research these words: *mantle, mountain/mountain of God, mandate, mission, and prophetic identity*. Reflect on the following areas and write your insights and revelations in your journal. Then complete this chart. (1Tim.4:15; Josh.1:8; Psa.1:2-3)		
<u>1. My Mantle</u> (Authority)	<u>2. My Mandate</u> (Responsibility)	<u>3. My Mission</u> (Assignment)
<u>4. My Mountains or Pillars</u> (Realms) (Education, Government, Arts and Entertainment, Family, Religion, Media, & Business)	<u>5. My Metron</u> (Territories)	<u>6. My Prophetic Identity</u> (Spiritual DNA)
<u>How These Six (6) Areas Relate to Each Other</u> (Alignment)		

Wisdom Nuggets
2 Timothy 1:6-7, 11-14

	FOR THE LEADER OR MENTOR	FOR THE PROPHET-IN-TRAINING
PRINCIPLES	List three (3) principles that you can learn from these scriptures.	List three (3) principles that you can learn from these scriptures.
PROTOCOLS	List three (3) protocols that you can learn from these scriptures.	List three (3) protocols that you can learn from these scriptures.
APPLICATION	How can you apply these principles and protocols personally and professionally as a leader or mentor?	How can you apply these principles and protocols personally and professionally as a prophet?

Module 3 Overview

The Purpose of God's Prophet

Objectives

In this module, participants will

1. Know the purpose of God's prophet.

2. Learn the principles of operating in the prophetic using scriptures.

3. Understand mantles and their distribution.

4. Identify biblical prophets' mantles, their mantles' distribution, and their conflict with worldly mantles.

5. Assess their own prophetic mantles and their distribution.

Key Terms

Mantle
Distribution
Purpose

Key Concepts

Know the Purpose of God's Prophet
Kingdom Mantle Distribution

Additional Concept
Kingdom Distribution Center

Key Scriptures

1Sam.10:1-12
1Kgs.19:19
2Kgs.2:9
2Kgs.4:1-7,10,13-17

Additional Scriptures
2Kgs.6:1-7
1Sam.1-31; 2Sam.1-24; 1Kgs.1-22
(Study throughout the course for principles
and protocols regarding prophets.)

Module 3 Lesson Structure

1. Begin with the following discussion questions:

    - What should be the impact of God's prophet in the church, the marketplace, and the world?

    - What would that impact look like?

2. Start Module 3 video.

3. Begin with prayer and time for participants to share their comments or testimonies. ***Note**: You can also use this time to have them share their feedback on the homework assignment. ***

4. Review the terms *prophet, nabi, hozeh*, and *chozeh*. Apostle Dwann gives a testimony related to the discussion.

5. Review Module 2 information regarding the purpose of the prophet.

6. Provide time for Q &A.

    - *1st Participant's Question:* What is the process of grooming a global prophet?
    - *2nd Participant's Question*: What happens when opposition breaks out in a public setting?

    *Mentions Moses and the sons of Korah and Aaron's rod budding among the others. Biblical References: Num.12, Num.16, Num. 17).

    ***Note:** Pause the video after the discussion on the second question. Read the scriptures on one of these instances of opposition and discuss insights, revelations, and proper protocols. ***

7. Introduce the topic: Know the Purpose of What God's Prophet Does.

8. Read and discuss 1Sam.10:1-12.

9. Provide time for participants to share testimonies.

10. Read and explain the principles concerning the purpose of what God's prophet does in 1Kgs.19:19, 2Kgs.2:9, & 2Kgs.4:1-7,10,13-17.

    ***Note:** During this discussion, a participant asks the following question. You may want to discuss it with your participants, too:

    - *Participant's Question*: Have you seen how those who are committed to you or who are familiar with your prophetic gift (i.e. family, etc.) take your gift for granted, but those who have never met you appreciate your prophetic gifting?

11. The module will end in the middle of discussing 2Kgs.4:13-17. You can provide time to continue the discussion on these scriptures and pull out more principles and protocols regarding the purpose of God's prophet.

12. Provide time for Q&A.

13. End with prayer.

14. Debrief the video.

Module 3 Assignment

Write a detailed, one-page report in which you respond to the following questions:

- *Assessing Distribution from Biblical Prophets' Mantles*
  Research three (3) prophets in the Bible. Identify their mantles and explain how they distributed from them. Share your insights and revelations.

- *Examining the Conflict between Kingdom and Worldly Mantle Distributions*
  Research Jezebel (1 Kings & 2 Kings) and Elijah (1 Kings). What insights and revelations can you learn about how kingdom mantles and their distribution come against worldly or demonic mantles in the earth? What is God's response throughout Jezebel's story? How does the battle between Elijah and Jezebel's prophets illustrate the principles of the purpose of God's prophet?

Rubric		
Criteria	Met the Criteria (Y)	Did Not Meet the Criteria (N)
• Identifies three (3) prophets and their mantles.		
• Explains how the prophets distributed from their mantles.		
• Shares their insights and revelations on their research.		
• Shares their insight and revelations on Jezebel's mantle and Elijah's mantle and connects them to the principles of the purpose of God's prophet.		
• Meets the 1-page requirement.		

Facilitation Strategies

*Then opened he their understanding,
that they might understand the scriptures.*
Luke 24:45

1. Have everyone, including yourself, discuss their mantles and how they distribute from them. Assess the effectiveness and the fruit of the distribution. How can you improve your mantle's distribution to better impact your church, city, or region?

2. There are distribution centers within our country that ship out different products from different industries. They assist in maintaining the flow of productivity and prosperity in commerce. Think about the concept of God's prophets as kingdom distribution centers. Discuss your insights and revelations on that concept. What should that kingdom distribution look like in the earth? How did the biblical prophets manifest as kingdom distribution centers?

3. You may want to assign the following supplemental exercise: *My Mantle's Distribution*.

4. You may want to complete the wisdom nuggets exercise together as a class or assign it as an individual activity.

My Mantle's Distribution

Directions: Reflect on your mantle and its distribution. Complete the following chart.
*Note: You may have more than one mantle. Write about each one.

My Mantle(s)	
How My Mantle Resembles the Patterns of Prophetic Mantles in the Bible	
How My Mantle Distributes	
My Assessment of Its Distribution	

Now reflect on your insights, revelations, and strategies about your responses to this exercise in your journal.

Wisdom Nuggets
2 Timothy 2:15,21

	FOR THE LEADER OR MENTOR	FOR THE PROPHET-IN-TRAINING
PRINCIPLES	List three (3) principles that you can learn from these scriptures.	List three (3) principles that you can learn from these scriptures.
PROTOCOLS	List three (3) protocols that you can learn from these scriptures.	List three (3) protocols that you can learn from these scriptures.
APPLICATION	How can you apply these principles and protocols personally and professionally as a leader or mentor?	How can you apply these principles and protocols personally and professionally as a prophet?

Module 4 Overview

Knowing the Purpose of Prophetic Protocol

Objectives

In this module, participants will

1. Know the purpose of prophetic protocol and understand its meaning.
2. Learn about prophetic companies and their organizational roles in the church.
3. Unpack the principles of prophetic protocol.
4. Complete a prophetic reflection.

Key Terms

Prophetic
Protocol
Prophetic Protocol
Proprietary
Precept
Prophetic Company
Prophetic Alert

Key Concepts

Prophetic Protocol
Prophetic Company Structure
Prophetic Organizational Models
Submission (as it relates to prophets)

Key Scripture

Eph.2:20

Module 4 Lesson Structure

***Note:
This module does not have presentation slides.
You will find the term definitions, organizational models,
and some of the principles listed for you in this section
and the Facilitation Strategies section. You may
want to provide them to your participants.

1. Begin with the following discussion questions:

    - What do you think a prophetic protocol is?
    - How should it operate in a ministry, church, or organization?

    *Based on their responses, assess where they are and what you need to emphasize during the lesson.

2. Start Module 4 video.

3. Begin with prayer and time for participants to share their comments or feedback about Module 3. *****Note:** You can also use this time to have them share their feedback on the homework assignment. ***

4. Introduce the module's topic: The Purpose of Prophetic Protocol.

5. Explain the meaning of the term *prophetic protocol*:

    - *Prophetic*: That which proceeds from the prophet's work and authority; as one who is an agent of the kingdom and as a prophet, everything that comes out of my work and from my dimension of authority is prophetic.
    - *Protocol*: A system of proprietary rules and precepts that governs activities.
    - *Prophetic Protocol*: A system of rules and regulations that govern the prophetic.
    - *Proprietary*: Privately owned and controlled.

- *Precept*: Commandment or direction given as a rule of action or conduct; standard directives, words of action or acting, words of conducting oneself in the prophetic office or as you are operating in the prophetic realm.

6. Discuss prophetic protocol from the perspective of a prophetic company and define prophetic company:

    - *Prophetic company*: A community of prophets who are members of a local church body or other organization whose primary purpose is to provide prophetic care, service, prophecy, and oversight to membership.

7. Ask the following discussion question:

    - After listening to the discussion on prophetic companies, how many of you think that you have been involved in one?

8. Address challenges of prophetic protocol and prophetic companies in churches.

9. Explain what prophetic companies do and how they fit into the organizational structure of the church. Mention shamar prophets, prophetic psalmists, and different levels within the prophetic company.

    - Resource: *The Shamar Prophet* by John Eckhardt

10. Provide time for Q & A.

11. Describe the structure of a prophetic company.

12. Provide time for discussion and comments on what has been discussed so far. Talk about to whom prophets should submit.

13. Cover principles of prophetic protocol individually.

    - *Principle 1:* Have your prophecies tested or judged within a prophetic company or someone in your circle.

    - *Principle 2:* Document your prophecies, dreams, and visions either through journals or digital recorders.

    - *Principle 3:* Submit your prophecies to senior leaders.

Module 4 Lesson Structure

***Note:**
This module does not have presentation slides.
You will find the term definitions, organizational models,
and some of the principles listed for you in this section
and the Facilitation Strategies section. You may
want to provide them to your participants.

1. Begin with the following discussion questions:

   - What do you think a prophetic protocol is?
   - How should it operate in a ministry, church, or organization?

   *Based on their responses, assess where they are and what you need to emphasize during the lesson.

2. Start Module 4 video.

3. Begin with prayer and time for participants to share their comments or feedback about Module 3. ***Note:** You can also use this time to have them share their feedback on the homework assignment. ***

4. Introduce the module's topic: The Purpose of Prophetic Protocol.

5. Explain the meaning of the term *prophetic protocol*:

   - *Prophetic*: That which proceeds from the prophet's work and authority; as one who is an agent of the kingdom and as a prophet, everything that comes out of my work and from my dimension of authority is prophetic.
   - *Protocol*: A system of proprietary rules and precepts that governs activities.
   - *Prophetic Protocol*: A system of rules and regulations that govern the prophetic.
   - *Proprietary*: Privately owned and controlled.

- *Precept*: Commandment or direction given as a rule of action or conduct; standard directives, words of action or acting, words of conducting oneself in the prophetic office or as you are operating in the prophetic realm.

6. Discuss prophetic protocol from the perspective of a prophetic company and define prophetic company:

    - *Prophetic company*: A community of prophets who are members of a local church body or other organization whose primary purpose is to provide prophetic care, service, prophecy, and oversight to membership.

7. Ask the following discussion question:

    - After listening to the discussion on prophetic companies, how many of you think that you have been involved in one?

8. Address challenges of prophetic protocol and prophetic companies in churches.

9. Explain what prophetic companies do and how they fit into the organizational structure of the church. Mention shamar prophets, prophetic psalmists, and different levels within the prophetic company.

    - Resource: *The Shamar Prophet* by John Eckhardt

10. Provide time for Q & A.

11. Describe the structure of a prophetic company.

12. Provide time for discussion and comments on what has been discussed so far. Talk about to whom prophets should submit.

13. Cover principles of prophetic protocol individually.

    - *Principle 1:* Have your prophecies tested or judged within a prophetic company or someone in your circle.

    - *Principle 2:* Document your prophecies, dreams, and visions either through journals or digital recorders.

    - *Principle 3:* Submit your prophecies to senior leaders.

- *Principle 4:* Find a prophetic mentor. When the student is ready, the teacher will appear.

- *Prophetic 5:* Know your prophetic mantle and what you are supposed to do.

- *Principle 6:* Know your prophetic assignment and why God has called you to a place.

- *Principle 7:* Be prepared to shift when God changes your assignment to a church, ministry, or organization.
    - Submit to the process of transitioning in and transitioning out to avoid being stuck. If you don't have peace about a situation, don't move.

14. Provide time for Q&A.

15. Share the vision for Global Institute of Church and Marketplace Prophets (GICMP).

16. Ask the following discussion questions:

    - Where do you see the absence of the prophetic or prophetic protocol in our ministry, church, or organization?
    - What can we do to address it?

17. Debrief the video.

18. End in prayer.

Module 4 Assignment

Write a detailed, one-page prophetic reflection explaining your responses to the following questions. Be prepared to share at the beginning of the next module.

- *Reflective Question 1*: Where are you in the prophetic?
- *Reflective Question 2*: Where are you supposed to be?
- *Reflective Question 3*: How are you going to get there?

Rubric		
Criteria	Met the Criteria (Y)	Did Not Meet the Criteria (N)
• Describes in detail where they are in the prophetic using specific examples.		
• Describes in detail where they are supposed to be in the prophetic using specific examples.		
• Explains how they are going to get there by stating specific goals, strategies, and action steps.		
• Demonstrates reflective thought on how the previous modules impact their prophetic journey.		
• Meets the 1-page requirement.		

Facilitation Strategies

*Then opened he their understanding,
that they might understand the scriptures.
Luke 24:45*

1. Decide how you want to transition into Prophetic Bootcamp 201. Preview the modules and determine if there are any specific activities you want them to do in preparation for the next set of lessons.

2. Have a conversation on the word *transition*: personally, biblically, and organizationally. What does successful and non-successful transition look like?

3. Discuss how prophetic companies could work in your church or organization.

4. There is no supplemental exercise or wisdom nuggets exercise for this module.

5. There are organizational charts on the following page.

Prophetic Protocol Organizational Model

Apostle

(Visionary)

Senior Pastor

(Partners with the Prophet; Shepherds the Congregation)

Senior Prophet or Prophetic Company Superintendent

(Oversees Prophetic Company)

Prophetic Company /Staff Prophets
(Serves as a prophetic covering and agents who help the vision flourish)

Prophetic Intercessors

(Interceding for the vision and supporting the prophets and the church in prayer)

Order of Submission for Prophets

Apostle

Apostolic Prophet

Senior Prophet

Prophetic Mentors

Mid-Course Reflection

Write your responses in your journal.

1. Find a quiet place, be still, listen, and meditate in the Holy Spirit's presence. What do you see? What do you hear? What do you discern?

2. What have been the strengths and areas of improvement in your facilitation so far? Where do you need to shift?

3. How have the modules developed you personally?

4. Think about your discussions on prophetic protocol and prophetic companies. What is God instructing you to do? How does He want you to implement prophetic protocol and prophetic companies?

5. Reflect on your participants' progress. What else do they need at this point?

6. Revisit your course vision. Is there anything you want to add, remove, or modify?

7. What are your other thoughts about the training?

PREPARING THE FACILITATOR TO LEAD:
FOCUS ON PROPHETIC BOOTCAMP 201

Module 5 Overview

Understanding Your Prophetic Status

Objectives

In this module, participants will

1. Review key concepts and reflections from Prophetic Bootcamp 101.

2. Learn about releasing basic and corporate prophecies.

3. Discern prophetically the current conditions of the world.

4. Understand the difference between prophets and psychics.

5. Explore the global ramifications of psychic shows and other worldly representations being broadcast over the various media outlets.

6. Defend how they are different and more valid than psychics.

Key Terms

Prophecy
Basic Prophecy
Corporate Prophecy
Purpose of Prophecy
Prophet
Psychic

Key Concepts

Releasing Basic and Corporate Prophecies
Difference Between Prophets & Psychics
Discerning What is Going on Prophetically in the World

Key Scriptures

2 Chr.20:13-20
Amos 3:7
1Kgs.13:11-26
1 Sam.9:7-9
1Cor.14:1-5
Isa.44:25

Module 5 Lesson Structure

***Note:
There are two videos for Module 5.
Part 1 is about 32 minutes long.
Part 2 is about 48 minutes long.
Plan accordingly for your sessions.

1. Begin with the following discussion questions:

   - What does it mean to be a prophet-in-training?

   - What would it look like?

   - Why do you think it is necessary for a person to start as a prophet-in-training instead of fully taking on the office of the prophet?

   *Based on their responses, assess where they are and what you need to emphasize during the module.

2. Start Module 5—Part 1 video.

3. Begin with prayer.

4. Go over the agenda.

5. Present three (3) reflective questions and invite current prophets-in-training to share where they are in their journey. *****Note:** You can have your participants share their Module 4 reflection assignment before or after this part. *******

6. Review prophetic scriptural foundations from Prophetic Bootcamp 101: 2Chr.20:20, Amos 3:7, 1Kgs.13:11-26, and 1Sam.9:7-16.

7. Explain that prophets should have a prophetic philosophy with specific scriptures as their foundation. Apostle Dwann shares her prophetic philosophy.

8. Review basic prophecy, the purpose of prophecy, and the terms *edify, exhort,* and *comfort* using 1Cor.14:1-5.

9. Discuss what basic prophecy is not.

10. Revisit how to release a basic prophecy.

11. Give specific examples of how to release a basic prophecy using scriptures to edify people in different scenarios.

12. Revisit the spiritual definition of prophecy.

13. Present 2Chr.20:13-20 as a biblical model for releasing a corporate prophecy.

14. Pause the video and ask your participants to read Isa.44:25. Discuss the following question:

    - What are your insights and revelations about this scripture?

15. Listen to the discussion of Isa.44:25.

16. Discuss the importance of assessing what's going on in environments and in the world.

17. Discuss current assessment of what is going on in the world. ***Note:** This video was originally recorded in 2012. Yet, God's word is not bound. Notice how these prophetic insights are probably still applicable to today's times. The video will stop in the middle of their discussion. ***

18. Ask the following discussion questions:

    - What is your assessment of what is currently happening in our world?
    - How are the current conditions similar or different to what is discussed in the video?
    - What is your assessment of what is currently happening in our church, organization, city, or state?

19. You will explain Module 5 assignment. It is not explained in this video, but the next video will have a discussion on their responses.

20. Debrief video.

Module 5 Lesson Structure (cont'd)

21. Begin Module 5—Part 2 video.

22. Continue to listen to the discussion on the current assessment of what is going on in the world.

23. Ask the following discussion question:

    - What other major takeaways do you have from their discussion?

24. Discuss Module 5 Homework Assignment. Ask your participants to share their responses to the homework. *****Note:** The video ends with the homework discussion. ***

25. Provide time for Q &A.

26. Debrief the video.

27. End in prayer.

Module 5 Assignment

Write a detailed, one-page report answering the following questions on the differences between prophets and psychics:

- *Current Global Spiritual Ramifications in Media*
  What is the GLOBAL SPIRITUAL RAMIFICATION of what is being broadcast via TV airwaves, music, or social media outlets?

- *Current Global Spiritual Ramifications of Psychics in Media*
  What is the GLOBAL SPIRITUAL RAMIFICATION of this show (*Long Island Medium* and/or any other psychic TV show) being broadcast via TV airwaves?

- *Defending Who You Are*
  As a Prophet, how would you explain WHO YOU ARE versus a PSYCHIC and WHY what you do is just as VALID or MORE VALID than that of a Psychic?

- *Counteracting Deception*
  As a Prophet, how would you propose to COUNTERACT this show (*Long Island Medium* or any other psychic TV show) and potential messages?

Rubric		
Criteria	Met the Criteria (Y)	Did Not Meet the Criteria (N)
• Gives the global ramifications of what is being broadcast over the various media outlets, including psychic TV shows like *Long Island Medium*.		
• Explains who they are versus a psychic and defends their validity over a psychic's validity.		
• Includes specific examples and scriptural references.		
• Meets the 1-page requirement.		

Facilitation Strategies

*Then opened he their understanding,
that they might understand the scriptures.*
Luke 24:45

1. After your participants share their Module 4 reflections, give feedback on where they are in the prophetic: beginner, intermediate, or advanced.

2. For Module 5 assignment, the original Question 1 and Question 2 have been revised for you.

3. Read Nehemiah 6:14 and its surrounding scriptures. Discuss Noadiah in the context of what you have learned in this module. What insights and revelations do you have about Nehemiah 6?

4. Here is a list of resources on the prophetic:

    - *Prophet, Arise* by John Eckhardt
    - *The Prophetic Advantage* by Michelle McClain-Walters

5. You may want to assign the following supplemental exercise: *Spirit of Truth Versus Spirit of Error*.

6. You may want to complete the wisdom nuggets exercise together as a class or assign it as an individual activity.

Spirit of Truth Versus Spirit of Error
1 John 4:1-6
Directions: Complete this chart.

Spirit of Truth (My Insights & Revelations)	How I Represent the Spirit of Truth	Spirit of Error (My Insights & Revelations)
	MY POSITION AS A PROPHET (Legislate & Intercede)	
	How I Stand Against the Spirit of Error	

TWO PILLARS THAT ARE PREVALENT IN OUR WORLD

YOUR MANDATE IS TO RELEASE THE SPIRIT OF TRUTH

<u>IN EVERY SITUATION AND ENVIRONMENT</u> AS GOD'S PROPHET!

Wisdom Nuggets
1 Timothy 3:1-12

	FOR THE LEADER OR MENTOR	FOR THE PROPHET-IN-TRAINING
PRINCIPLES	List three (3) principles that you can learn from these scriptures.	List three (3) principles that you can learn from these scriptures.
PROTOCOLS	List three (3) protocols that you can learn from these scriptures.	List three (3) protocols that you can learn from these scriptures.
APPLICATION	How can you apply these principles and protocols personally and professionally as a leader or mentor?	How can you apply these principles and protocols personally and professionally as a prophet?

Module 6 Overview

Prophesy Like a Prophet

Objectives

In this module, participants will

1. Review key concepts and reflections from Prophetic Bootcamp 101.

2. Learn about the principles and protocols of entering the next dimension.

3. Practice giving the Word of the Lord to each other and listen to examples.

4. Understand the spiritual relevance of quantum physics.

5. Develop a prophetic philosophy.

Key Terms

Corporate Prophecy
Dimension
Shift
Quantum Physics
(Spiritual Point-of-View)

Key Concepts

Prophesying Like a Prophet
Giving the Word of the Lord
Entering the Next Dimension

Key Scriptures

Gen.28:12
John 1:51
1Kgs.17:1 & 1Kgs.18:41-46

Module 6 Lesson Structure

Guest Instructor:
Prophet LaTonya C. Smith, Simply Latonya Kingdom Ministries

***Note:
There are two videos for Module 6.
Part 1 is about 51 minutes long.
Part 2 is about 31 minutes long.
Plan accordingly for your sessions.

1. Start Module 6—Part 1 video.

2. Begin with prayer.

3. Go over the agenda.

4. Listen to praise reports of prophetic release and share important nuggets from last session. *****Note:** You may want to pause the video and have them to share as well. *******

5. Present another review of basic concepts from Prophetic Bootcamp 101. *****Note:** With each review comes fresh revelation. It is suggested that you do not skip this part. *******

6. Give a more detailed discussion about how to release a corporate prophecy using 2Chr.20:13-20.

7. Have participants practice giving each other the Word of the Lord. Listen to examples. *****Note:** After you listen to this exercise and the examples, pause the video, and give your participants an opportunity to practice. *******

8. Ask participants to reflect on the following questions as Prophet LaTonya explains the principles and protocols of entering the next dimension:

    - What makes a prophet's prophecies shift situations?
    - How can you use your mantle to distribute someone's situation to another dimension?

9. Discuss the principles and protocols of entering the next dimension. Reference scriptures: Gen.28:12; John 1:51. *****Note:** The video will end after her discussion. *******

10. Debrief the video.

11. End with prayer.

12. Have students write in their journals about insights and revelations from this video.

Module 6 Lesson Structure (cont'd)

13. Begin Module 6—Part 2 video.

14. Provide time for Q &A and continue to share principles and protocols of entering the next dimension.

15. Explain the homework assignment.

16. End with prayer.

17. Debrief the video.

18. Ask the following discussion question:

    - What major takeaways do you have from this video?

Module 6 Assignment

Develop and write a detailed, 1-page prophetic philosophy in which you will respond to the following questions using several scriptural examples in your discussion. Be prepared to share.

Foundational scripture: 2Chr.20:20

- *Your Foundation*
  What foundational principles based on the Word of God does your prophetic ministry stand on?

- *Your Prophetic Charge*
  What has God ordained for your prophetic ministry to illuminate about the prophetic?

- *Your Call to Dismantle*
  What negative elements in the earth realm has God called you to de-construct utilizing your prophetic mantle?

- *Your Understanding of the Prophetic*
  Briefly account for "what the prophetic is" and what the prophetic isn't".

Rubric		
Criteria	Met the Criteria (Y)	Did Not Meet the Criteria (N)
• States and explains the foundational, scripture-based principles on which their prophetic ministry stands.		
• Discusses what God has ordained their prophetic ministry to illuminate about the prophetic.		
• Describes the negative elements in the earth realm that God has called them to deconstruct using their prophetic mantle.		
• Meets the 1-page requirement. • Shares the prophetic philosophy in class.		

Facilitation Strategies

*Then opened he their understanding,
that they might understand the scriptures.
Luke 24:45*

1. Share your prophetic philosophy as a model for your participants.

2. Offer time outside of scheduled sessions to give assistance on the assignment. Let them know that they will continue to work on this assignment in Module 7 and Module 8. No other assignments will be given. After this module, there will be no more supplemental exercises or wisdom nuggets exercises. Their focus should be on their prophetic philosophy.

3. Discuss other biblical examples of prophets entering the next dimension.

4. Here is a list of resources on the prophetic ministry in the marketplace & prophetic assessment:

    - *The Global Call to Marketplace Ministry* by Dwann Holmes
    - *Assessing Your Prophetic Self* by Paula Price, Ph.D.

5. You may want to assign the following supplemental exercise: *My Prophetic Philosophy Planning Guide*.

6. You may want to complete the wisdom nuggets exercise together as a class or assign it as an individual activity.

My Prophetic Philosophy Planning Guide

My Insights and Revelations from the Holy Spirit

Before you begin filling out this planning guide, go to a quiet place and listen to God's voice. Write in your journal and then complete the planning guide below.

Now in the morning, having risen a long while before daylight,
He went out and departed to a solitary place; and there He prayed.
Mark 1:35 (NKJV)

My Prophetic Ministry		
My Foundational Principles	**My Foundational Scriptures**	**How They Represent My Prophetic Ministry**
Prophetic Illuminations Flowing Through My Prophetic Ministry	**How I See Them Flowing**	**Where They Are Flowing**
Negative Elements My Prophetic Mantle Will De-construct		
What the Prophetic Is		
What the Prophetic Is Not		

Wisdom Nuggets
2 Timothy 2:22-26 & 2 Timothy 4:1-8

	FOR THE LEADER OR MENTOR	FOR THE PROPHET-IN-TRAINING
PRINCIPLES	List three (3) principles that you can learn from these scriptures.	List three (3) principles that you can learn from these scriptures.
PROTOCOLS	List three (3) protocols that you can learn from these scriptures.	List three (3) protocols that you can learn from these scriptures.
APPLICATION	How can you apply these principles and protocols personally and professionally as a leader or mentor?	How can you apply these principles and protocols personally and professionally as a prophet?

Module 7 Overview

Prophetic Consecration for Prophetic Preparation

Objectives

In this module, participants will

1. Understand the key terms: prophetic consecration, prophetic preparation, and suffering.

2. Learn about the principles and protocols of giving a Word to the Body.

3. Receive important nuggets from Apostle Dwann and Prophet LaTanya.

4. Listen to a senior prophet give insight on suffering and consecration.

5. Continue developing their prophetic philosophy.

Key Terms

Prophetic Consecration
Prophetic Preparation
Suffering

Key Concepts

Prophesying a Word for the Body
Putting Suffering in the Proper Perspective
Principles & Protocols of Prophetic Consecration & Preparation

---

Module 7 Lesson Structure

1. Begin with the following discussion questions:

    - What questions do you have about the prophetic philosophy?
    - What do you think prophetic consecration means?
    - Why do prophets go through a greater level of suffering?

    *Based on their responses, assess where they are and what you need to emphasize during the lesson.

2. Start Module 7 video.

3. Begin with prayer.

4. Go over the agenda.

5. Provide time for praise reports regarding prophetic increase.

6. Discuss questions and goals and share most important nuggets.

7. Listen to a senior prophet share her insights about suffering and consecration.

8. Explain how to give a Word for the Body.

9. Present principles and protocols for cleansing and consecration.

10. Provide time for Q & A and additional sharing of prophetic principles.

11. End in prayer.

12. Debrief the video.

Facilitation Strategies

*Then opened he their understanding,
that they might understand the scriptures.
Luke 24:45*

1. Share your insights and experiences with prophetic preparation, prophetic consecration, suffering, and giving a Word for the Body. Do you know of any other senior prophets who can give their testimonies?

2. Decide if you want to give more practice in prophesying basic or corporate prophecy or giving a Word of the Lord or a Word for the Body.

3. You may also want them to give you or the spiritual leader of your church or organization a Word of the Lord. Record each word and judge it. If the Word of the Lord is for your spiritual leader, release the recordings to him or her.

4. How are you going to handle prophetic consecration for preparation with your participants?

5. No supplemental exercises or wisdom nuggets exercises.

Module 8 Overview

Developing Your Prophetic Philosophy

Objectives

In this module, participants will

1. Learn additional prophetic principles and protocols through class discussion and insights from seasoned prophets.

2. Share their prophetic philosophies and receive feedback.

3. Review next steps in prophetic development and ministry goals.

Key Terms

Kingdom Initiative
Prophetic Kingdom Ambassador
Seven (7) Pillars of Society

Key Concept

Final Prophetic Principles and Protocols

Key Scriptures

1Chr.12:32
Gen. 49

Module 8 Lesson Structure

1. Begin with the following discussion questions:

    - What has been the most inspiring during these eight (8) sessions?
    - What has been the most challenging?
    - What is your biggest accomplishment during this course?

    ***Note:** Share your responses to the questions as well. ***

2. Start Module 8.

3. Begin with prayer.

4. Go over the agenda.

5. Share important nuggets and testimonies and discuss questions and goals.

6. Have participants present their prophetic philosophies and receive feedback.
   ***Note:** Pause the video at different intervals. Have your participants share their prophetic philosophies and give your feedback. ***

7. Provide time for Q & A.

   - *Participant's Question*: Since you mentioned your call to the marketplace, have you come up with any plan as it relates to your next step in ministry to enhance the prophetic call on your life or your prophetic mantle?

8. Reference and elaborate on prophetic principles found in 1Chr.12:32 & Gen. 49.

9. Explain kingdom initiative as it relates to their prophetic mantle. Ask them how they will impact the Kingdom of God as a Prophetic Kingdom Ambassador.

10. Challenge them to create five (5) to ten (10) year goals that should be executed in phases, benchmarks, and measurable outcomes.

11. Discuss the wealth initiative.

12. Encourage them to continue to reflect on these questions:

    - Where are you in the Prophetic?
    - Where are you supposed to be?
    - How are you going to get there?

13. Provide time for Q & A and course wrap up.

14. End with prayer.

15. ***Note:** Check to see if the 30-minute introductory call is still available. ***

16. Debrief the video.

Facilitation Strategies

*Then opened he their understanding,
that they might understand the scriptures.*
Luke 24:45

1. Consider scheduling your own 30-minute prophetic conferences with your participants.

2. Prophesy a Word of the Lord over each participant. Make sure they record it on their phones. Enlist your seasoned prophets to assist you.

3. Share your final nuggets of insight and wisdom. Be transparent in answering the final three (3) reflective questions.

4. Brainstorm and discuss actions steps for moving forward.

5. Devise a special way to celebrate: Congratulations, you have completed your prophetic journey!!!

6. Here is a list of additional prophetic resources:

   - PAQ (Prophetics Assessment Questionnaire) by Paula Price
   - GICMP Ordination Track
   - GICMP *School of Prophetic Intercession* course
   - GICMP Prophetic Convocation
   - GICMP Prophetic Prayer Explosion

Facilitator's Evaluation

Write your responses to the following questions in your journal.

1. What are your major takeaways from the training?

2. What went well during your facilitation?

3. What are some areas of improvement in terms of facilitation?

4. What do you wish you could have done differently?

5. What kind of feedback did you receive from your participants?

6. What changes would you make to the mode of facilitation?

7. Did you try any of the facilitation strategies, supplemental exercises, and/or wisdom nuggets exercises? How did they go? Which ones would you adapt?

8. How well did you maintain your focus on your vision during the training?

9. How well did you meet your goals and prayer targets?

10. How well did you align your training to your core values?

Final Reflection

Write your thoughts in your journal.

1. Find a quiet place so you can hear God's voice. Ask Him for direction on moving forward with your ministry, church, or organization. Write what you see and hear.

2. Reread your first reflection and your mid-course reflection. What has changed since you have written them? How have you grown spiritually? Reflect on your facilitation journey and record your thoughts.

MEET DWANN HOLMES

 ABC, NBC, CBS, NPR

I'M Dwann Holmes to some and Pastor Dwann to others and MEDIA GURU to MOST!

I help BOSS LADY - FOUNDERS of FAITH create COMPREHENSIVE MEDIA LAUNCHES so that they CAN MAINTAIN THEIR MEDIA VISION AND BUILD THEIR Million Dollar BRAND ON-DEMAND

I started off as a TV News Reporter/Anchor back in 1994 then opened a Faith-Friendly TV Production Company back in 2000 that transformed into an Ad Agency while living in Nashville, Tennessee.

Was even named one of EBONY MAGAZINE's 30 FUTURE LEADERS of AMERICA back in 2000!

Now, I call Jacksonville, Florida home and Mentor, Teach, Train & Affirm those called to Prophetic Ministry, ENTREPRENEURSHIP AND MEDIA.

I've won lots of journalism awards, been nominated for a few Emmys, and most recently made my way to the top of Amazon's Best Sellers.

For BOSS LADY FOUNDERS OF FAITH we are the leading MEDIA DESIGN AGENCY that provides CREATIVE BRANDING ON-DEMAND. Unlike MANY, we MEET DESIGN DEADLINES, ON-TIME, EVERY-TIME!

When it comes to CREATIVE DESIGN, MY clients hire me TO MAINTAIN THEIR BRANDS and help with their yearly project launches.

I am excited and grateful to use my gifts and talents to clean up media mess, relieve stress and get them on track to launch their media projects on-time with excellence.

For the last 22 years I've used a proprietary process called [BRAND ON-DEMAND that helps my clients MAINTAIN THEIR PROVEN BRAND & CREDIBILITY with EXCELLENT CREATIVE DESIGN that helps them LAUNCH new projects and initiative on-time, every time, as we BRAND ON-DEMAND

GET UNLIMITED
WEEKLY GRAPHIC DESIGNS FOR
(1) MONTHLY AFFORDABLE INVESTMENT !!!

TEXT **877.595.9117** WITH QUESTIONS · CHURCHDESIGNSNOW.COM

Dwann Holmes
Media Expert - Trainer - Author - Prophetic Mentor

www.ingramcontent.com/pod-product-compliance
Lightning Source LLC
Chambersburg PA
CBHW080913170426
43201CB00017B/2315